a first book of
numbers

Chez Picthall

picthall and gunzi

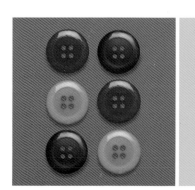

Created and produced by
Picthall & Gunzi Limited
21ᴀ Widmore Road
Bromley BR1 1RW
United Kingdom

Editor: Margaret Hynes
Designer: Paul Calver
DTP: Tony Cutting & Ray Bryant
Educational consultants: Diana Bentley, MA Advanced Diploma in Children's Literature, & Jane Whitwell, Diploma in Special Educational Needs
Photography: Steve Gorton & Andy Crawford
Wildlife photography: Jane Burton
Production: Lorraine Estelle
Editorial Director: Christiane Gunzi

ISBN 978-1-907604-10-2

Reproduction by Colourscan in Singapore
Printed and bound by Wing King Tong in China

Picthall & Gunzi wish to thank the following people and organizations for their invaluable help with the production of this book:

Lucia Allen, Jane Burton at Warren Photograph, Margaret Darby, Molly Ellington, Aliyah Green, Lewis Hawkins, Christopher Hinson at Eight by Four, Peter Picthall, Yuki Price, Amber Sayers, Lily Smith, Susan Stowers, Anthony Stubbs, Jesse Tyrell

Picture credits: Courtesy of **Swatch Watches** p.16; Courtesy of **Getty Images**: AJA Productions p.25, Peter Cade p.25, Jim Cummins p.25; Courtesy of **Sony UK** p.27; Courtesy of **Lawrence Manning/Corbis** p.25; Courtesy of **Jane Burton** p.21, p.26

Contents

Notes to parents & caregivers

A *First Book of Numbers* was created for young children with the help of educational experts and parents, and provides an exciting introduction to the world of counting and numbers. With the help of interactive questions and specially-devised games and puzzles, this unique first maths book will help parents, caregivers and teachers explore all the key basic maths concepts with children under seven years. By creating an environment that encourages communication, A *First Book of Numbers* builds essential skills in the areas of number recognition and language development.

This colourful, entertaining first numbers book is a valuable way to help your child become familiar with the basic concepts of mathematics. All the essential elementary maths concepts are covered, including counting, matching, shapes, patterns, sequencing and calculating.

A *First Book of Numbers* has been designed to develop a child's awareness in a naturally progressive way. As you progress through the book, the concepts become more complex and more challenging. Special "skills symbols" at the top of each page will help you to identify and reinforce each of the key maths concepts.

Key maths skills

123	Counting
Ⅲ/	Sequencing
↗	Connections
⊞	Patterns
▲	Matching
↕	Relationships
±	Calculating
⏳	Shapes
◎	Space
⫿⫿	Measures

The skill symbols at the top of the pages will help you to identify which maths concepts are covered by the activities on that page.

Using this book

When looking through this book with your child, it is important to create a relaxed atmosphere, allowing the child to set his or her own pace. Try to give plenty of encouragement and praise, and always finish on a positive note. By encouraging youngsters to have fun with numbers and counting, you will help to build their confidence and will encourage them to enjoy mathematics.
As you work through the pages together, ask your child to look beyond the book too, and ask him or her to guess how many things he or she can see. Talk about numbers that you encounter in everyday life, and those numbers that are special to the child, such as his or her age, house number, phone number or shoe size. Remember, the most effective way for children to learn about maths and numbers is through play. However you choose to use this book, there are many hours of entertainment and learning to be shared. Have fun!

Challenging interactive questions at the top of the pages link spoken and written numbers.

Skills symbols at the top of each page identify all the maths skills covered on the page.

Let's all share!
Count the children!
Are there more children than teddy bears?

Lily   Anthony   Jesse   Amber
Aliyah   Yuki   Lucia   Lewis

musical instruments   teddy bears   marbles

18

How many more masks do the children need?
Can every child have a car?
Are there more balls than children?

toy animals   chalks   masks
balls   cars

19

Specially-devised games and puzzles make basic maths fun for young children.

Tiny, colourful objects corresponding with every page number give little fingers extra things to seek, find and count.

Bright, colourful photographs of familiar objects engage children's interest.

Count from 1 to 10!

Let's count the hats!
How many pink cakes are there?

1 doll

2 cats

3 presents

4 ice lollies

5 hats

6 cakes

6

Can you count the shells?
How many of the sandcastles have yellow flags?
Count the flowers!

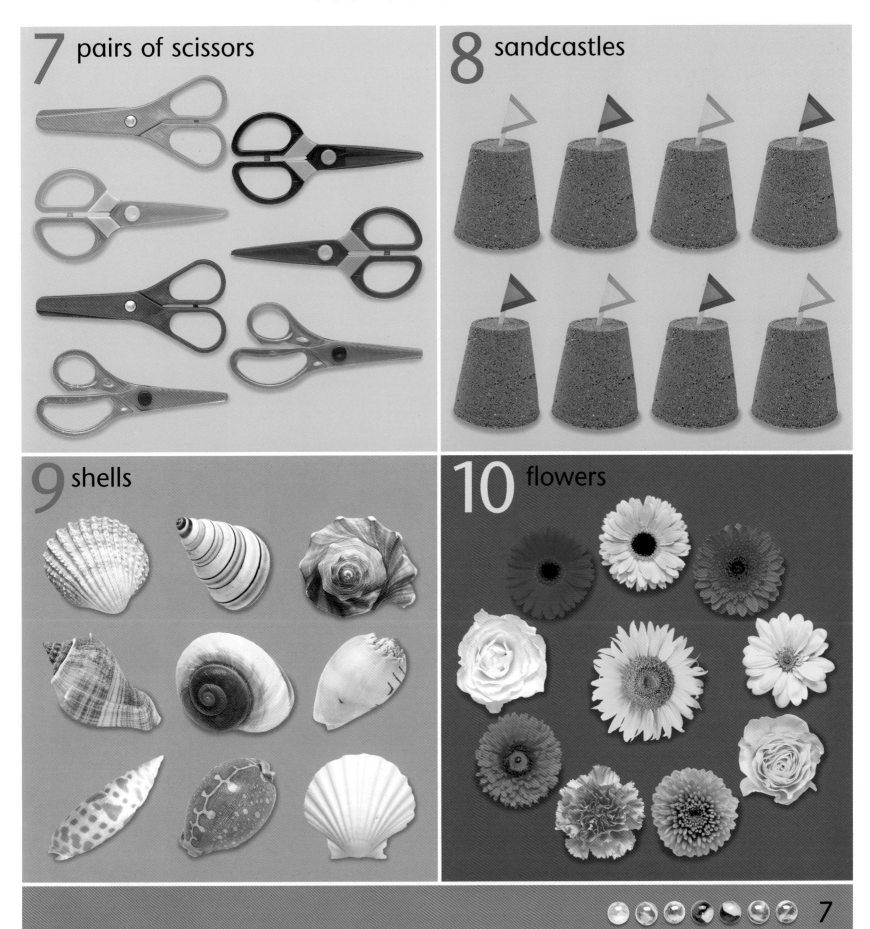

7 pairs of scissors

8 sandcastles

9 shells

10 flowers

Count from 11 to 20!

Let's count up to 20!

How many toy cars can you see?

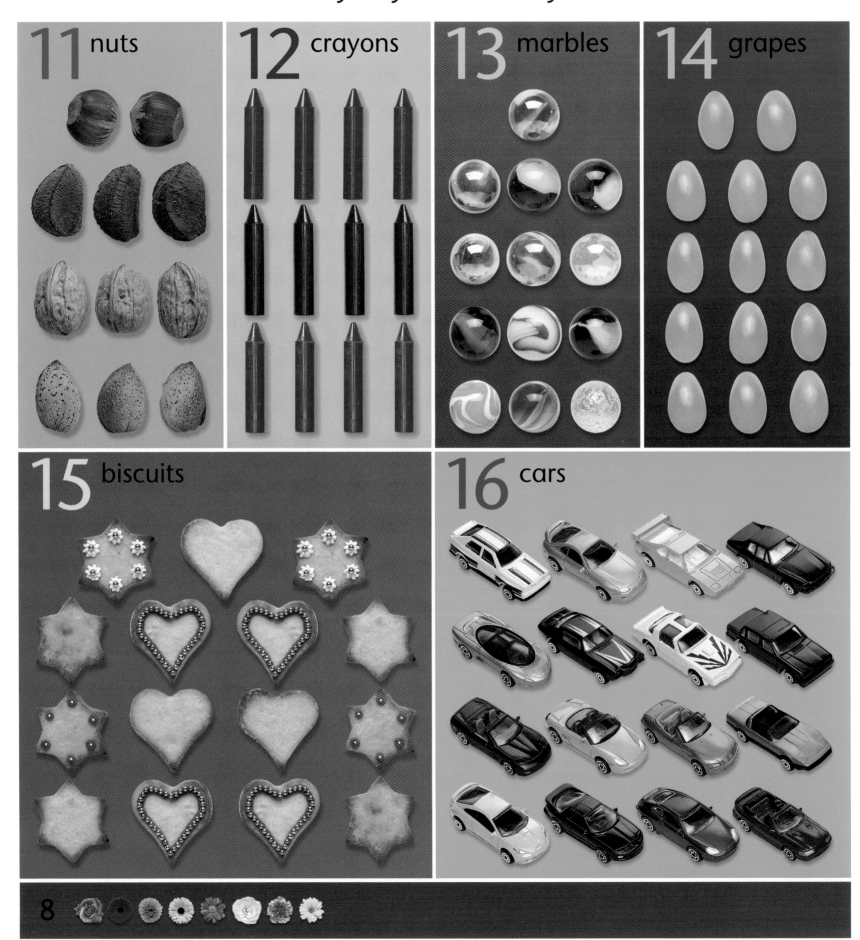

11 nuts

12 crayons

13 marbles

14 grapes

15 biscuits

16 cars

Can you count the juicy strawberries?
Count the green buttons!
How many sweets can you count?

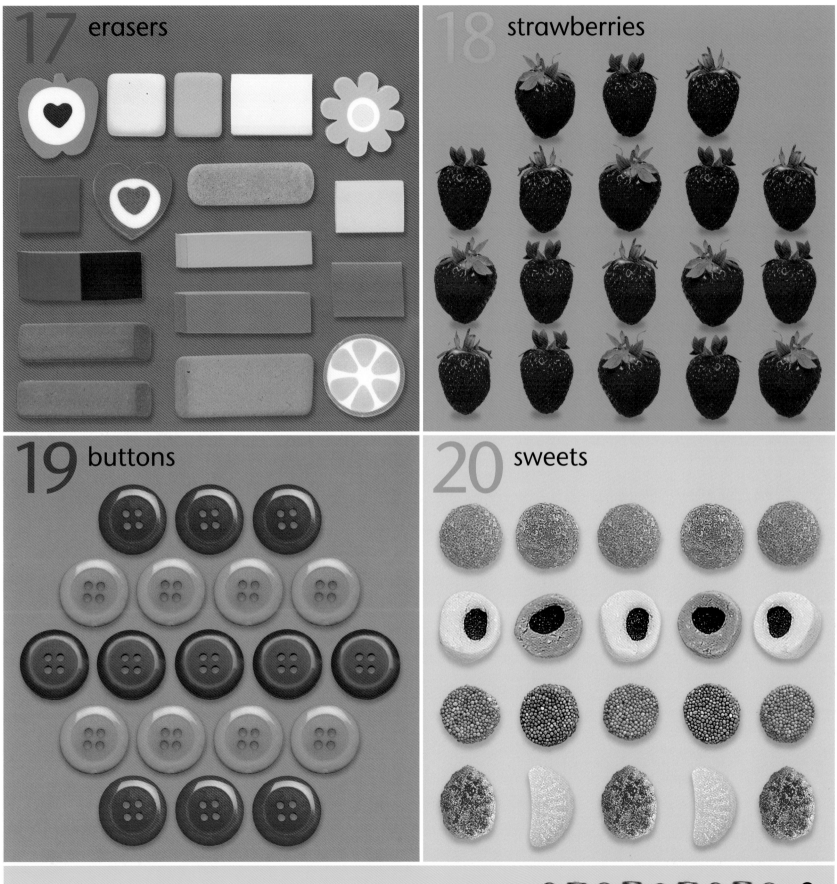

17 erasers

18 strawberries

19 buttons

20 sweets

Matching numbers

Count and match the numbers with the objects!
Do any of these numbers go with the bunch of keys?

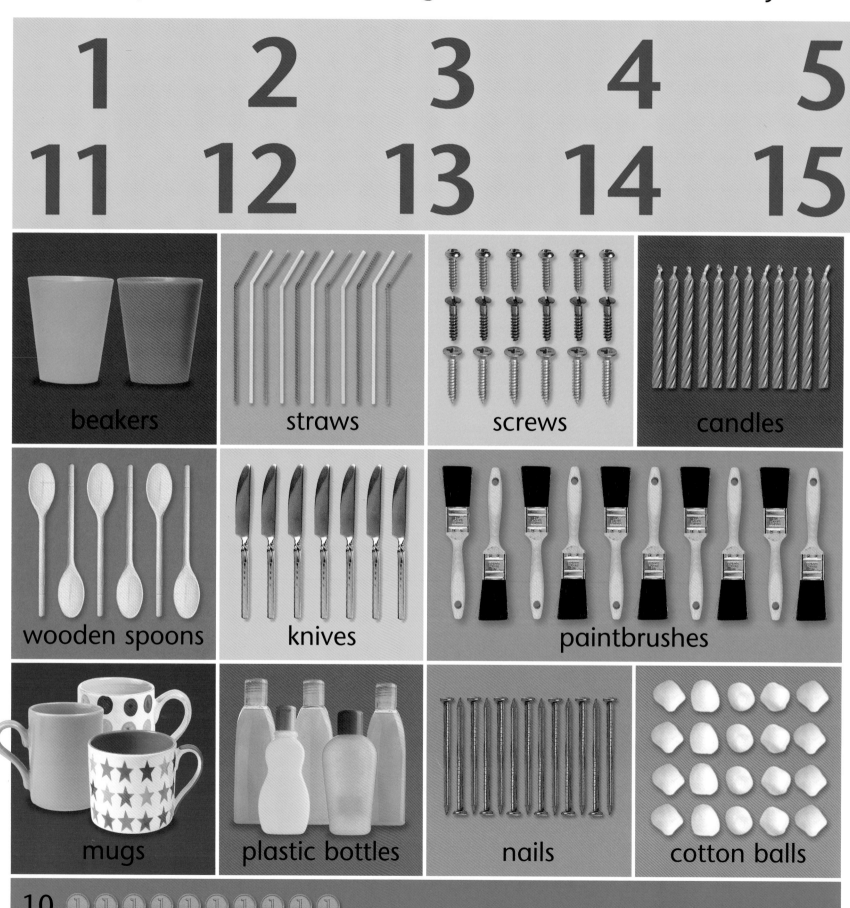

1   2   3   4   5
11   12   13   14   15

beakers

straws

screws

candles

wooden spoons

knives

paintbrushes

mugs

plastic bottles

nails

cotton balls

What number goes with the toothbrushes?
Can you find the group of 16 things?
Point to the number that goes with the screwdrivers!

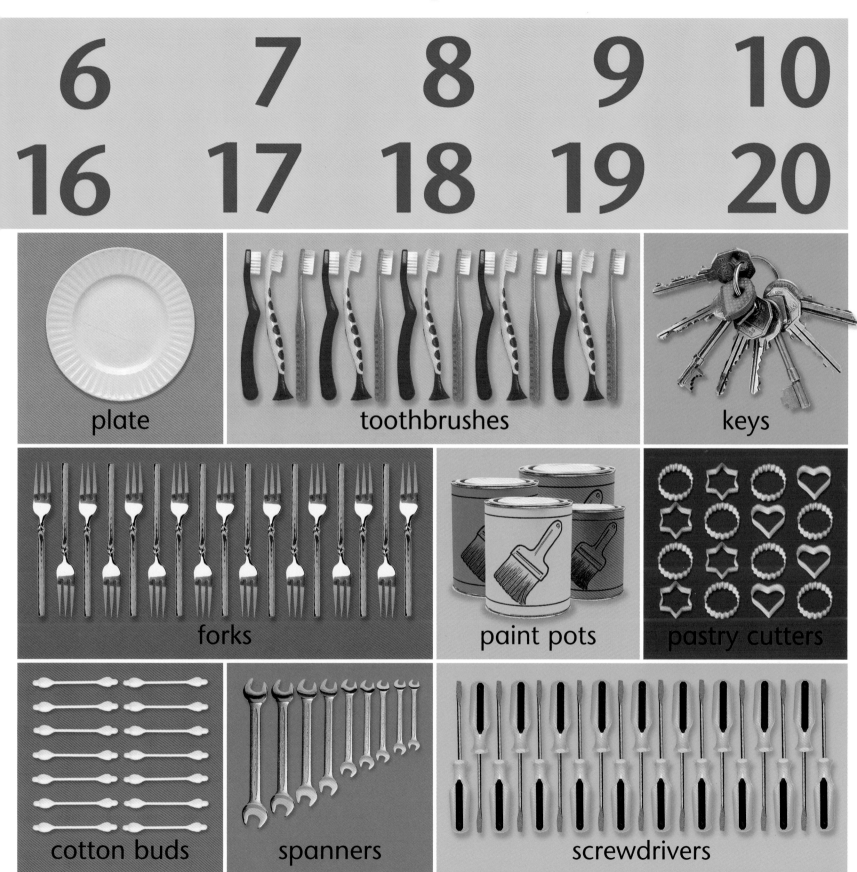

6   7   8   9   10
16   17   18   19   20

plate

toothbrushes

keys

forks

paint pots

pastry cutters

cotton buds

spanners

screwdrivers

Let's find numbers!

Find the numbers 4 and 19!
Can you see a group of 13 things?

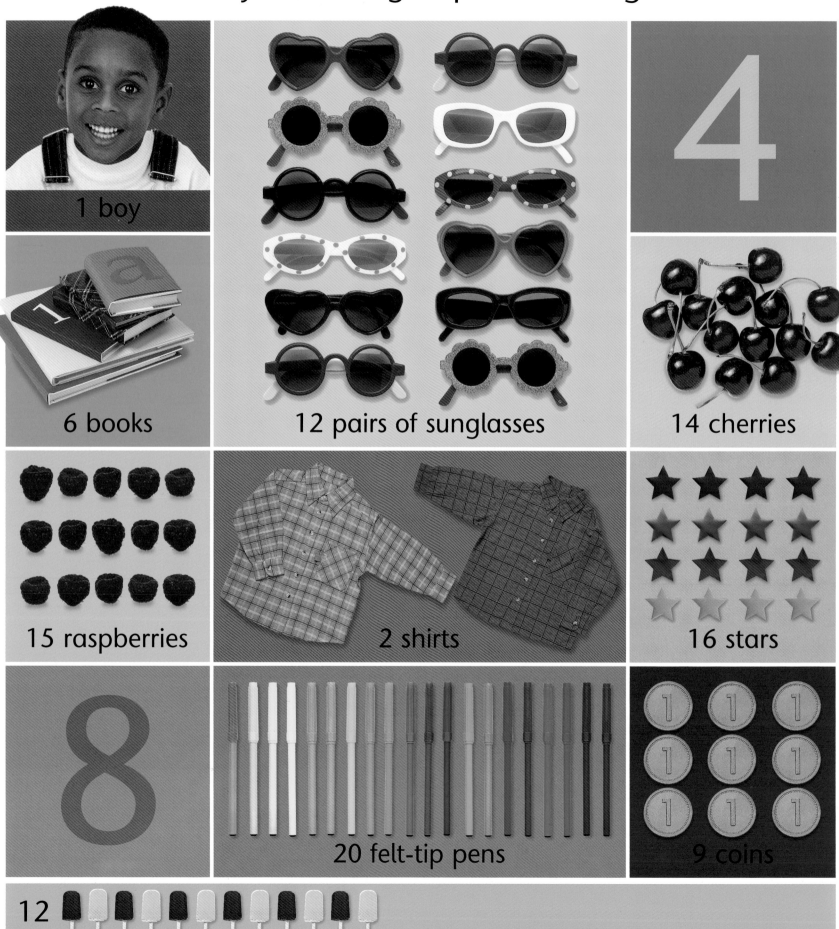

1 boy

6 books

12 pairs of sunglasses

4

14 cherries

15 raspberries

2 shirts

16 stars

8

20 felt-tip pens

9 coins

12

Can you find the numbers 8 and 11?
Point to the biggest number!
How many things are there in each group?

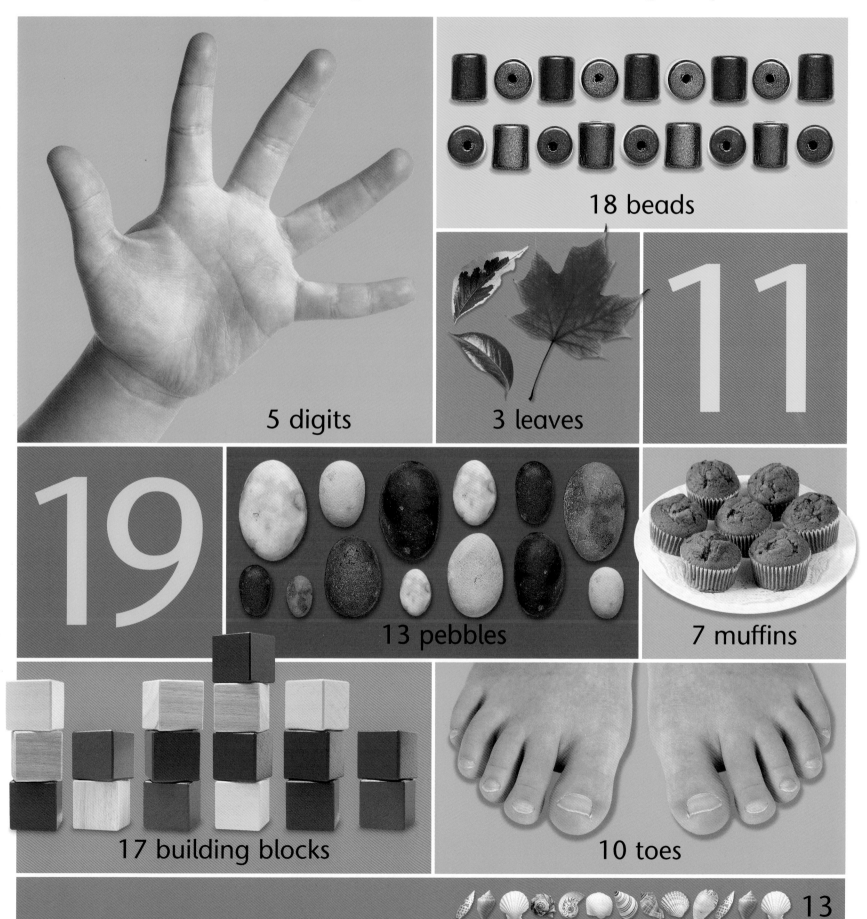

5 digits

18 beads

3 leaves

11

19

13 pebbles

7 muffins

17 building blocks

10 toes

Getting dressed

What clothes do you put on first?
Is your hat the third thing that you put on?

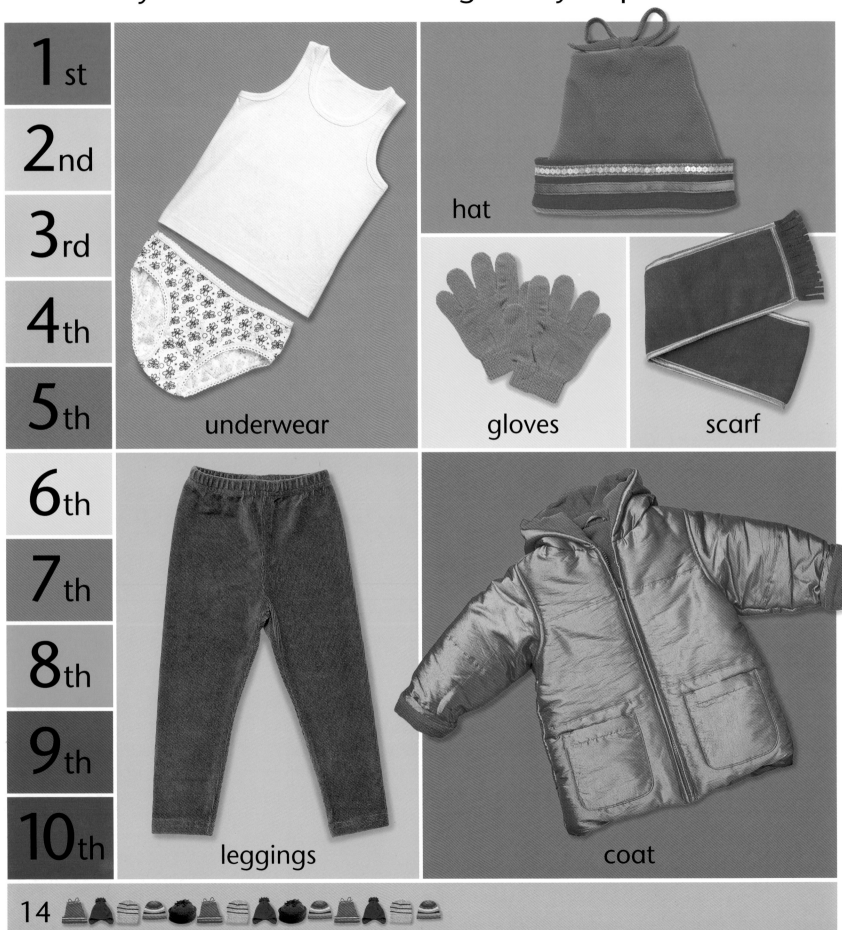

1st
2nd
3rd
4th
5th
6th
7th
8th
9th
10th

hat

underwear

gloves

scarf

leggings

coat

What clothes do you put on before your boots?
What clothes do you put on after your coat?
In which order do you put on your clothes?

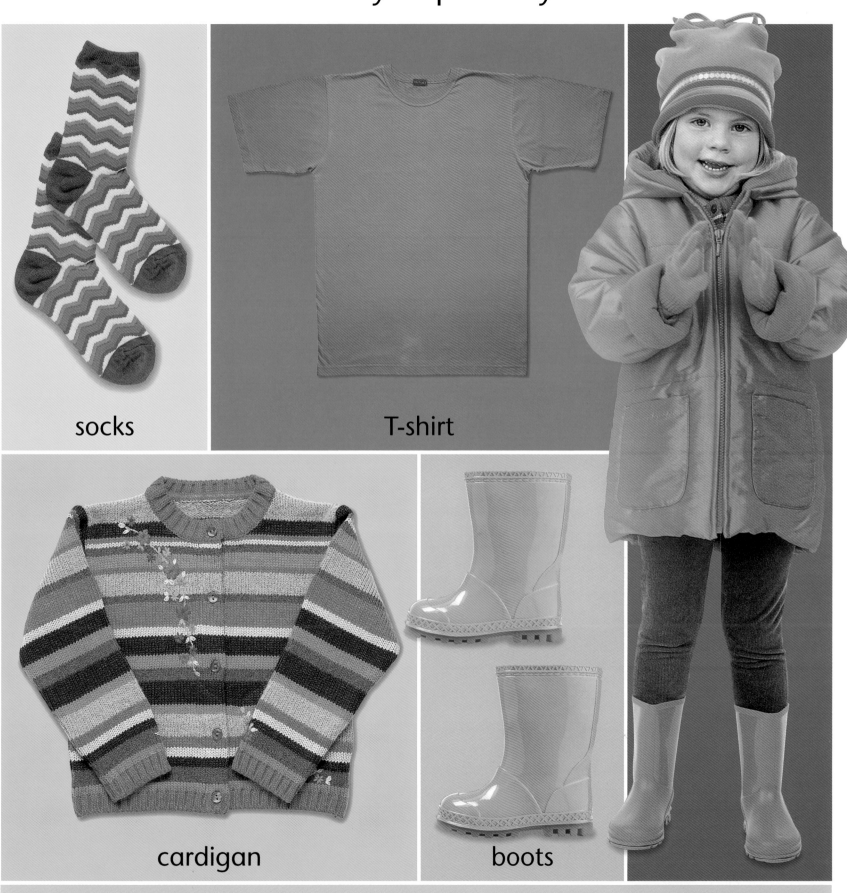

socks

T-shirt

cardigan

boots

Spot the missing numbers!

What number is missing on the telephone?
How many other missing numbers can you find?

clocks

ruler

watch

telephone

calendar

Jumbled numbers

Put these different things in the right order!
Can you count backwards from 5?

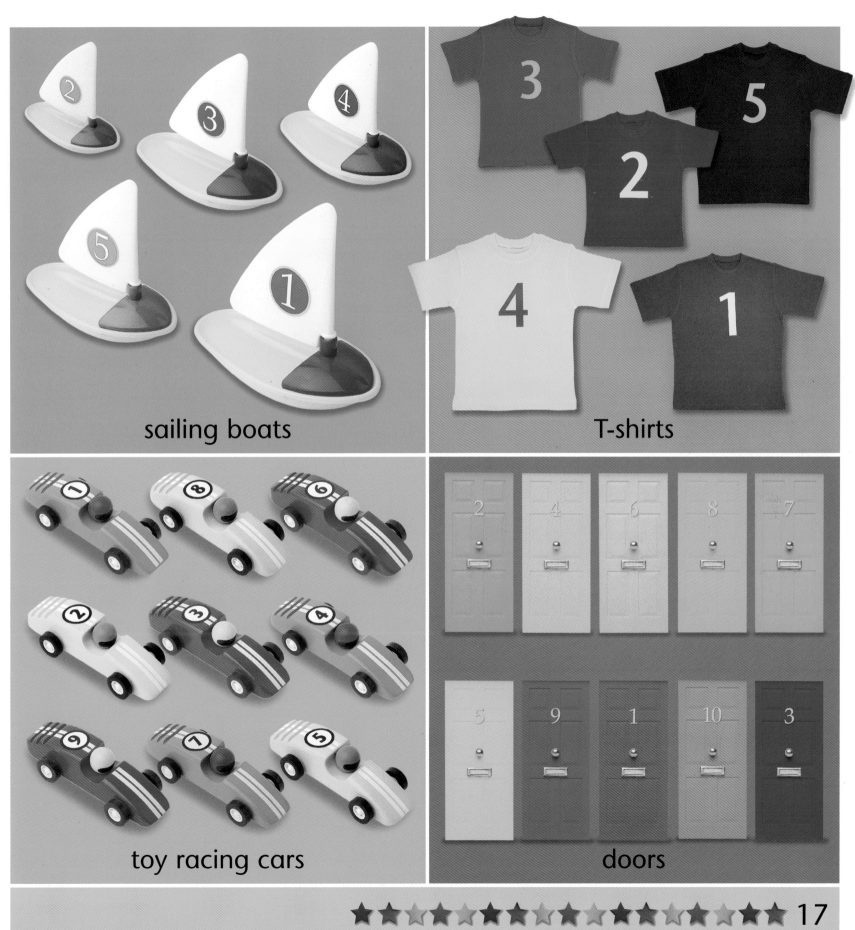

sailing boats

T-shirts

toy racing cars

doors

Let's all share!

Count the children!
Are there more children than teddy bears?

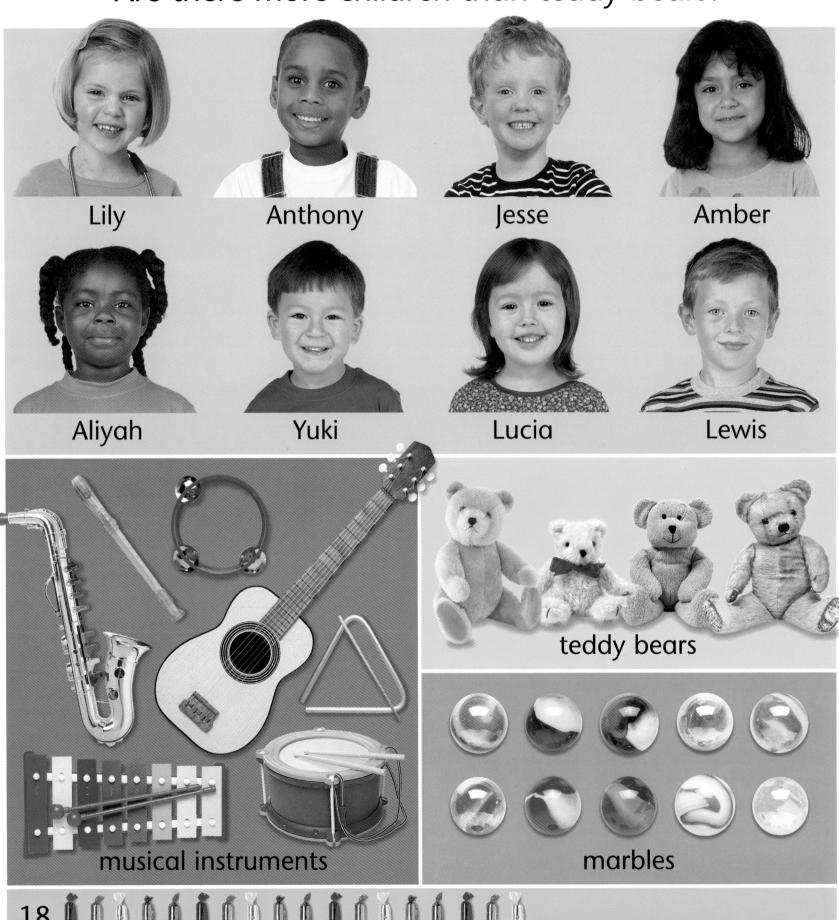

Lily

Anthony

Jesse

Amber

Aliyah

Yuki

Lucia

Lewis

teddy bears

musical instruments

marbles

How many more masks do the children need?
Can every child have a car?
Are there more balls than children?

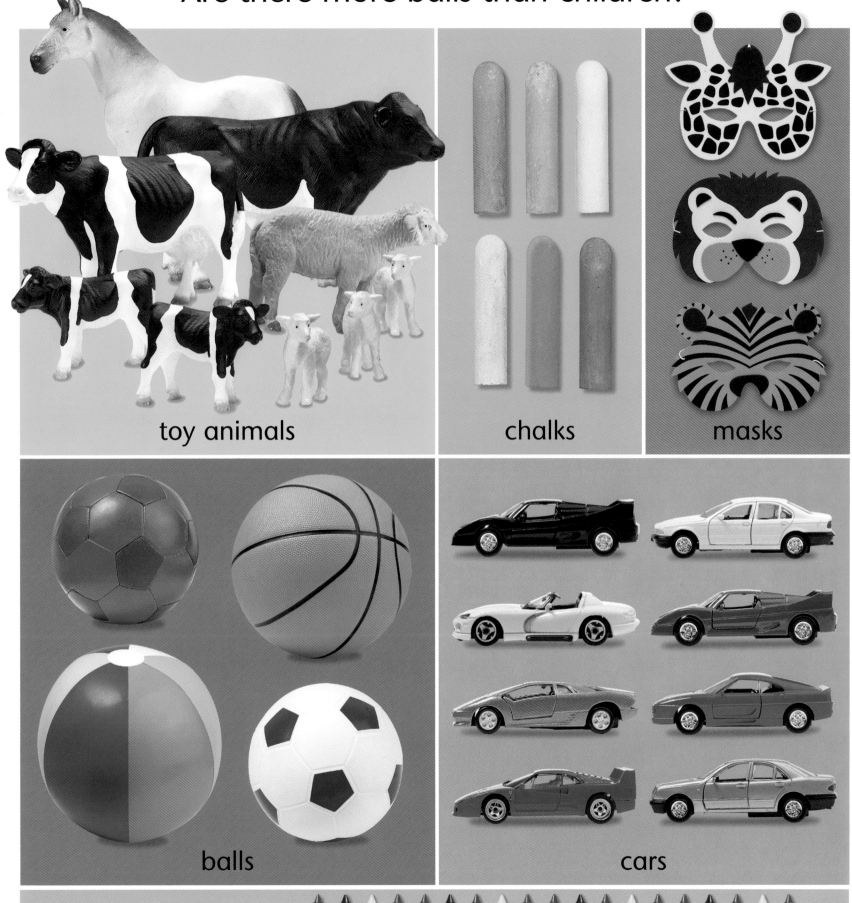

toy animals

chalks

masks

balls

cars

Party time!

How many cakes are there altogether?
Who has the most things to eat?

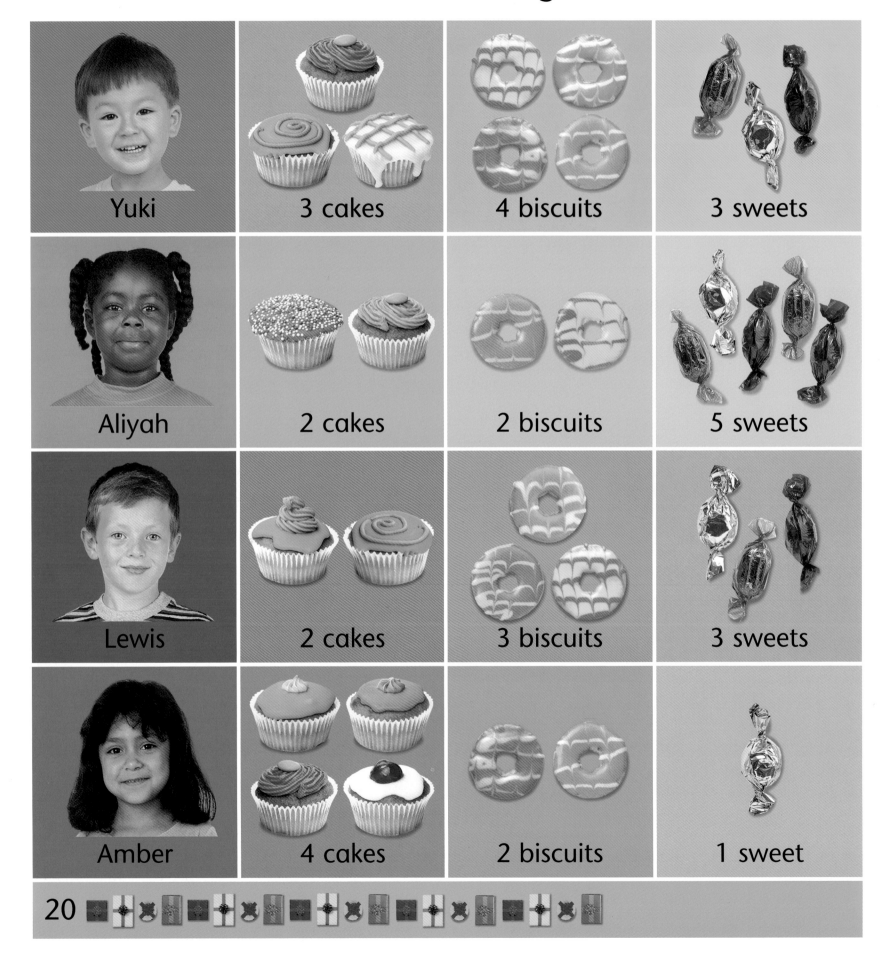

Yuki	3 cakes	4 biscuits	3 sweets
Aliyah	2 cakes	2 biscuits	5 sweets
Lewis	2 cakes	3 biscuits	3 sweets
Amber	4 cakes	2 biscuits	1 sweet

Baby animals

Who has the most babies?
Are there fewer kittens than baby rabbits?

The dog has 3 puppies

The cat has 5 kittens

The rabbit has 6 baby rabbits

The duck has 8 ducklings

Matching pairs
Point to both of the twins!
Can you match all of the pairs?

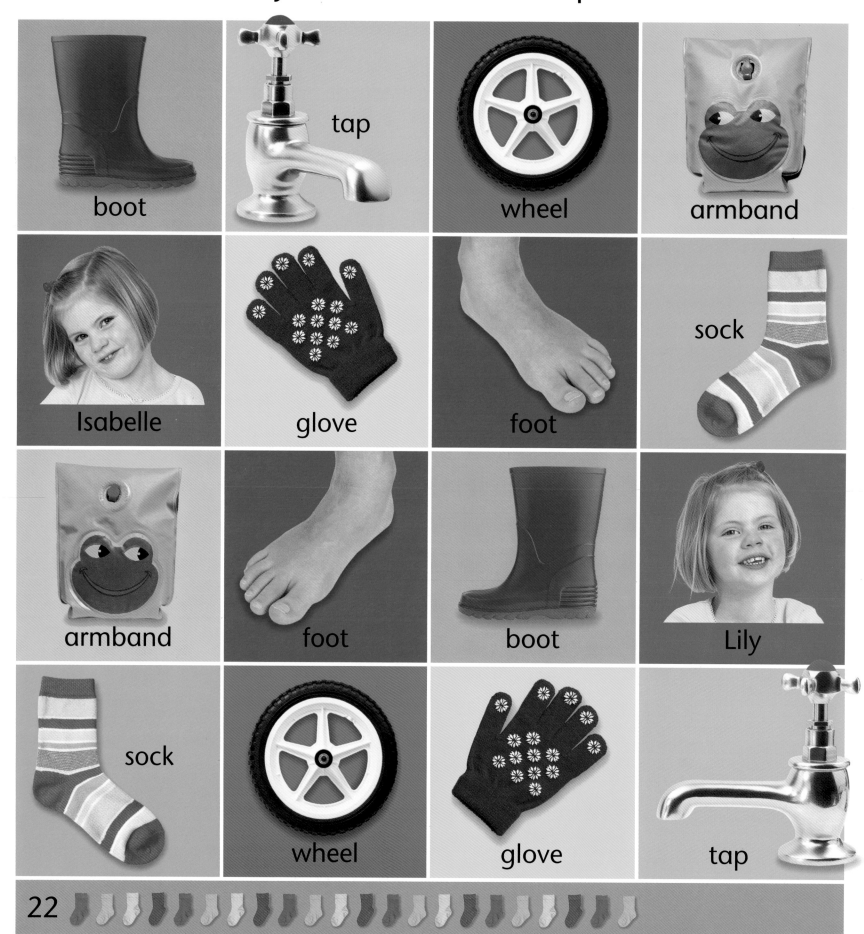

boot

tap

wheel

armband

Isabelle

glove

foot

sock

armband

foot

boot

Lily

sock

wheel

glove

tap

Counting in pairs
Count the pairs in each group!
How many shoes are in the group that has 5 pairs?

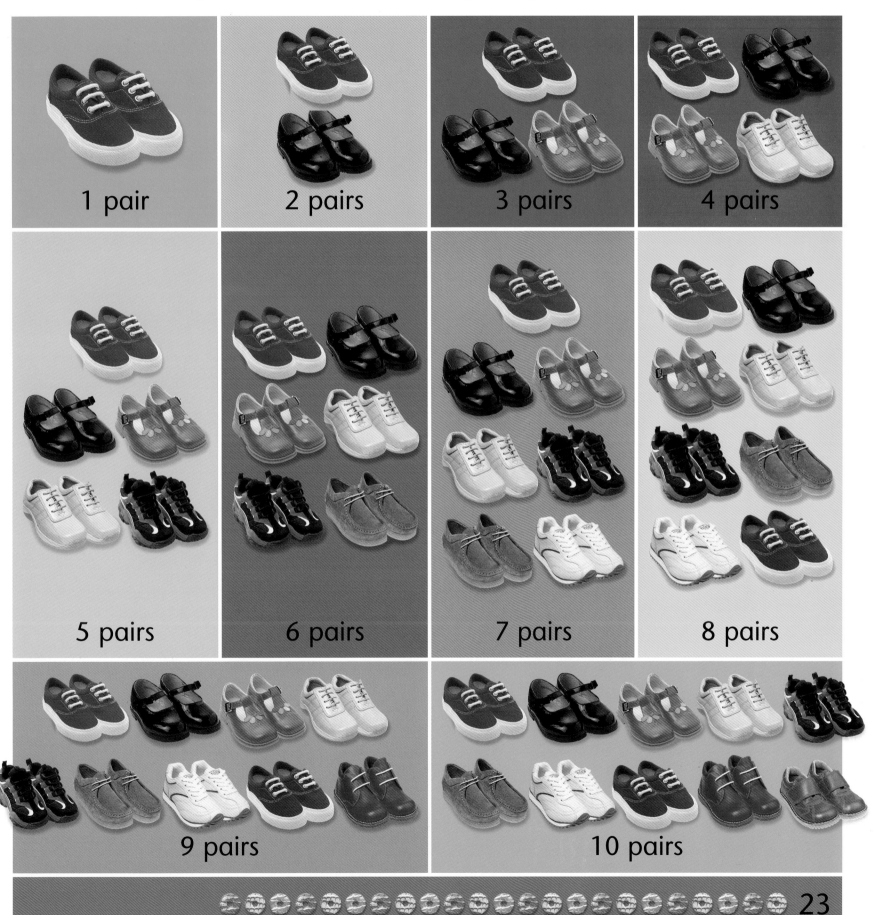

1 pair

2 pairs

3 pairs

4 pairs

5 pairs

6 pairs

7 pairs

8 pairs

9 pairs

10 pairs

Things that go together
Which of these things go together?
What goes with the bucket?

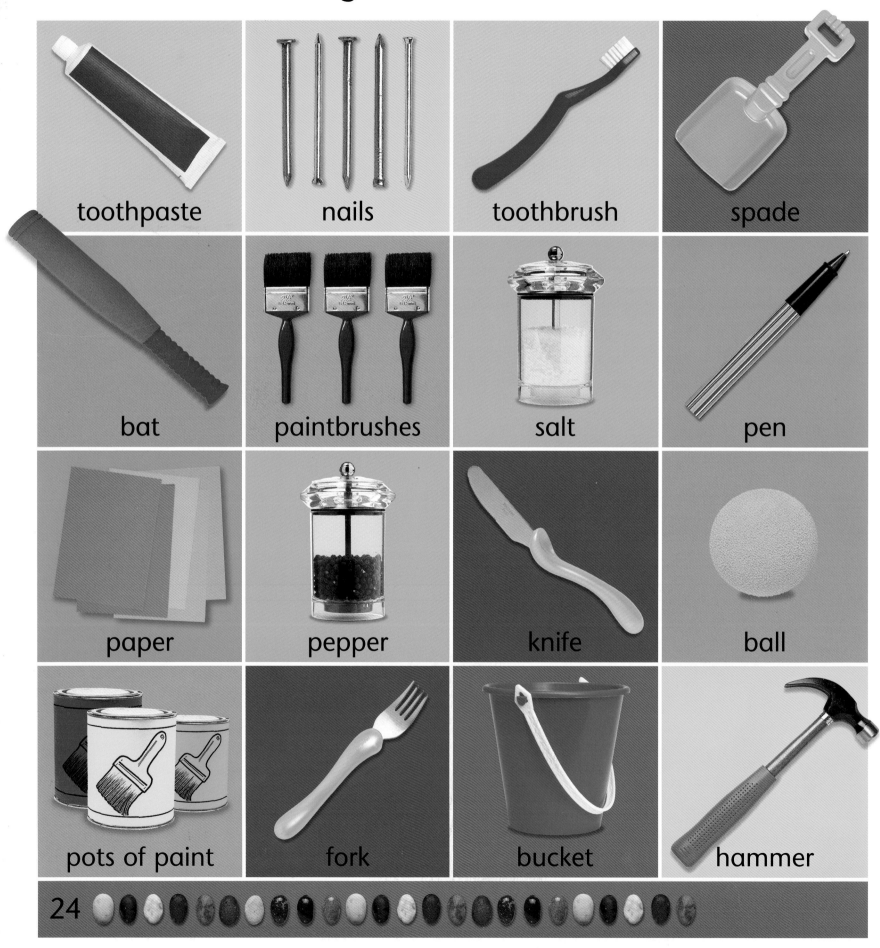

toothpaste

nails

toothbrush

spade

bat

paintbrushes

salt

pen

paper

pepper

knife

ball

pots of paint

fork

bucket

hammer

My day

At what time of day do you use these things?
When do you eat your breakfast?

morning

daytime

evening

night-time

skipping rope

pillow

toy train

juice

bread

towel

soap

cereal

sponge

bicycle

quilt

pyjamas

Odd ones out

Point to the odd ones out!

How many odd ones out are there?

puppies

blocks

cars

flowers

shirts

cakes

Is the tambourine the odd one out?
Where does the carrot belong?
Which group does the strawberry belong to?

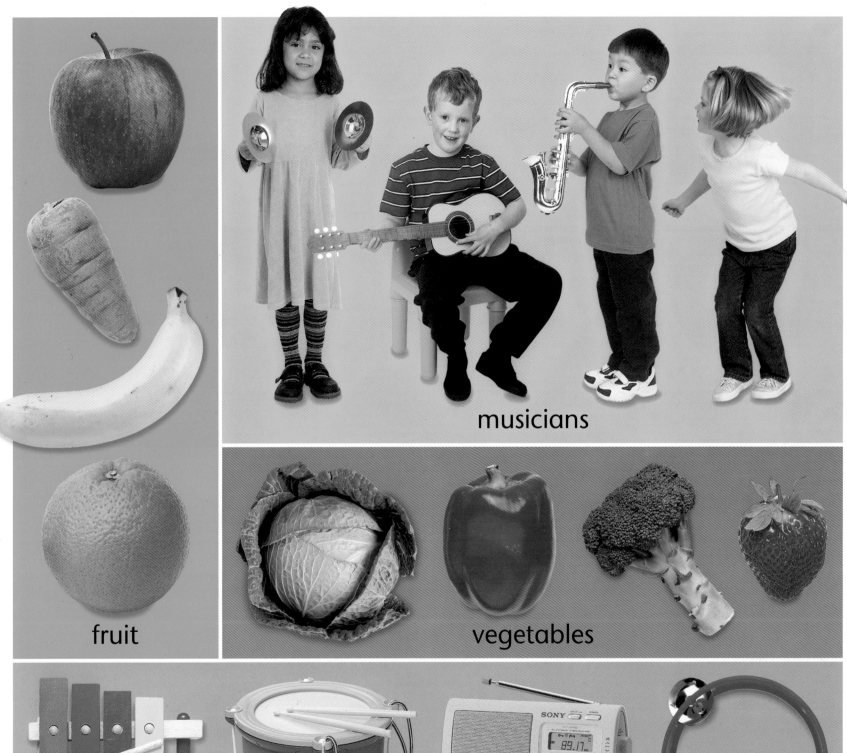

musicians

fruit

vegetables

musical instruments

Discovering shapes

Say the names of all the flat shapes!
Which of these shapes are solid?

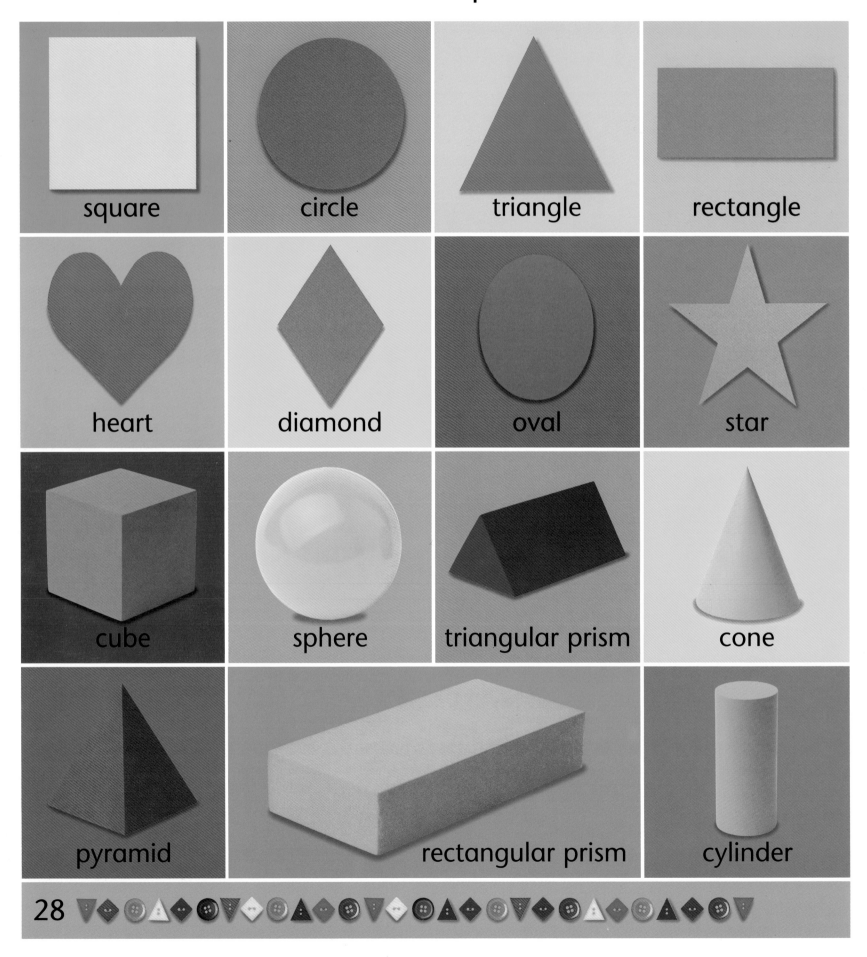

square

circle

triangle

rectangle

heart

diamond

oval

star

cube

sphere

triangular prism

cone

pyramid

rectangular prism

cylinder

What shape is the kite?
Can you match the objects to the shapes?
Can you find the cone-shaped object?

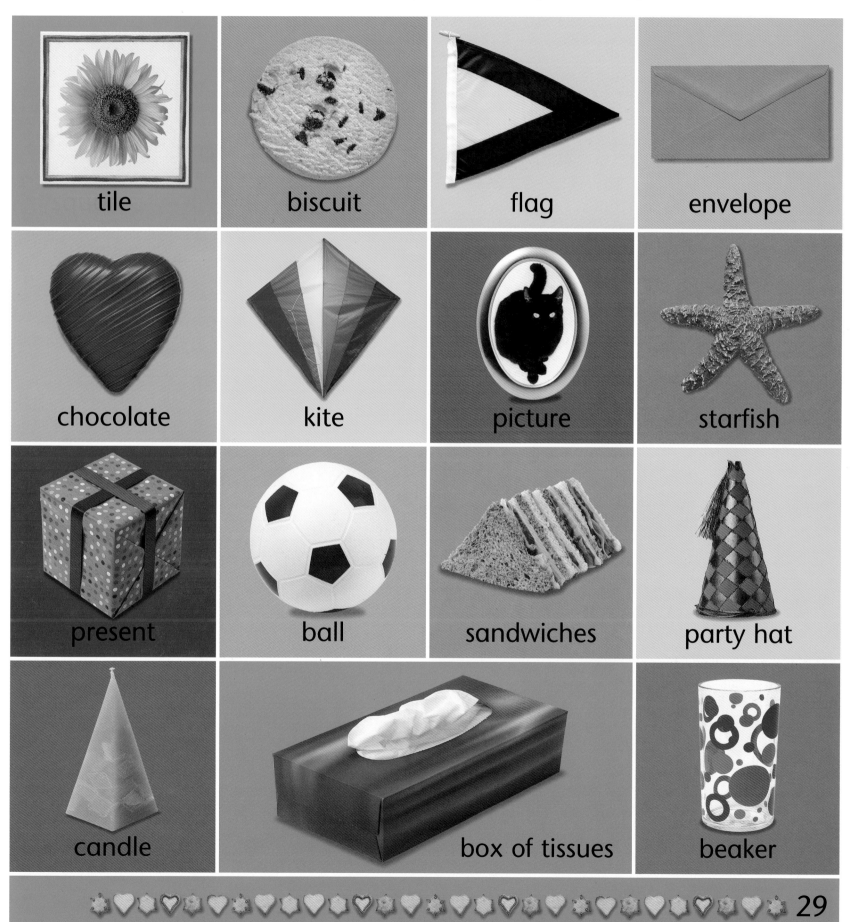

tile

biscuit

flag

envelope

chocolate

kite

picture

starfish

present

ball

sandwiches

party hat

candle

box of tissues

beaker

Spot the opposites!

Can you match all of the opposites?
What is the opposite of empty?

long

short

heavy

light

short

big

small

tall

full

empty

Where are they?

Where are all the dolls?

Where are all the teddy bears?

inside the box

outside the box

in front of the house

behind the house

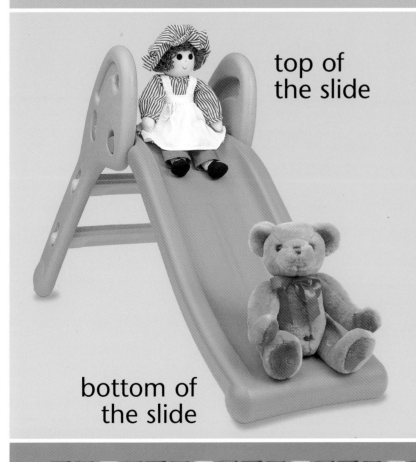

top of the slide

bottom of the slide

on the table

under the table

Making patterns and shapes

Call out the colours of the beads on the bracelet!
What different shapes can you see on this page?

What colour should the last carriage in this row be?

Which bead should replace the white bead on the bracelet?

Which shapes make the rectangle, big square and circle complete?

Which shape do you think comes next in this sequence?